Teaching English for Academic Purposes

Ilka Kostka and Susan Olmstead-Wang

English
Language
Teacher
Development
Series

Thomas S. C. Farrell,
Series Editor

Typeset in Janson and Frutiger
by Capitol Communications, LLC, Crofton, Maryland USA
and printed by Gasch Printing, LLC, Odenton, Maryland USA

TESOL Press
TESOL International Association
1925 Ballenger Avenue
Alexandria, Virginia 22314 USA

Publishing Manager: Carol Edwards
Cover Design: Tomiko Breland
Copyeditor: Tomiko Breland

TESOL Book Publications Committee
John I. Liontas, Chair
Robyn L. Brinks Lockwood, Co-chair   Guofang Li
Margo DelliCarpini   Gilda Martinez-Alba
Deoksoon Kim   Adrian J. Wurr
Ilka Kostka

Reviewer: Robyn L. Brinks Lockwood

ISBN 9781942223368

Contents

About the Authors

Ilka Kostka is a faculty member in the Global Pathways and American Classroom programs in the College of Professional Studies at Northeastern University, where she teaches ESL. Her research interests include second language academic writing and textual borrowing.

Susan Olmstead-Wang teaches advanced academic writing at the Johns Hopkins University School of Advanced International Studies (SAIS) and trains teachers for the University of Alabama–Birmingham, Master's in TESOL Program, via online and blended delivery.

Series Editor's Preface

The English Language Teacher Development (ELTD) Series consists of a set of short resource books for English language teachers that are written in a jargon-free and accessible manner for all types of teachers of English (native and nonnative speakers of English, experienced and novice teachers). The ELTD series is designed to offer teachers a theory-to-practice approach to English language teaching, and each book offers a wide variety of practical teaching approaches and methods for the topic at hand. Each book also offers opportunities for teachers to interact with the materials presented. The books can be used in preservice settings or in in-service courses and can also be used by individuals looking for ways to refresh their practice.

Ilka Kostka and Susan Olmstead-Wang's book *Teaching English for Academic Purposes* explores different approaches to teaching EAP and the various challenges this may present to a language teacher. Ilka and Susan provide a comprehensive overview of how to plan and teach EAP in an easy-to-follow guide that language teachers will find very practical for their own contexts. Topics covered include needs assessment, developing general academic skills, working with academic texts, listening and speaking, grammar, vocabulary, and blended skills. *Teaching English for Academic Purposes* is a valuable addition to the literature in our profession.

I am very grateful to the authors who contributed to the ELTD Series for sharing their knowledge and expertise with other TESOL professionals, because they have done so willingly without any compensation to make these short books affordable to all language teachers throughout the world. It is truly an honor for me to work with each of these authors as they selflessly gave up their valuable time for the advancement of TESOL.

Thomas S. C. Farrell

1

Introduction

We begin this book by sharing a few commonly held beliefs about academic English. We have heard students say that academic English is a "harder" or "better" version of English, and that they feel intimidated by it. We have also heard students say that they want to learn "long fancy words," which they believe are valued in academic language. Some students have said that they had to achieve a particular score on an English entrance exam, which they felt was more important than going to their English classes. And in writing courses, other students have stated that they did not feel like they had anything valuable to contribute to scholarly dialogue, saying, "I haven't published, so I have nothing new to say."

False beliefs about academic English prevail, and you may have heard others that we have not mentioned. But why do students feel that mastering academic English is difficult? Is it really so different from other types of English? In the chapters that follow, we hope to present academic English as a particular type of English that is not necessarily "better," "fancier," or "harder"; rather, it is simply a different *kind* of English. It is a kind of English that is usually learned in scholastic settings after general English has been acquired. We prefer to think of learning academic language as developing a set of skills that can be honed with practice, effective instruction, and motivation.

What Is EAP?

English for academic purposes (EAP) shares many common elements with English language teaching that occurs in other settings and in its parent field, English for specific purposes (ESP). However, the main distinguishing factor among these is that the pedagogical agenda of EAP is focused specifically on the formal teaching and learning of academic language. As a result, EAP scholarship includes pedagogical materials and design, classroom and academic discourse, academic genres, and teaching and administration in academic settings. Students in EAP settings typically have very specific goals for themselves, such as obtaining a university degree, and are highly motivated to achieve them.

The field of EAP has blossomed over the past two decades, largely due to the increase in students studying at English-medium universities, as well as the increase of English in scholarly publication, though not without controversy (for more on this topic, see Canagarajah, 1999). A wide variety of teaching materials and research related to the teaching and learning of academic English now exists, which has spurred a greater need for trained EAP teachers. We should note, however, that while EAP primarily focuses on students in secondary and postsecondary settings, scholarship in EAP also addresses the needs of older children and immigrants, who can benefit from specific academic instruction to facilitate their entrance into an English-dominant academic system (Hyland & Hamp-Lyons, 2002).

Our Approach to Teaching EAP

Because our readers may teach in varying settings across the world, we aim to present an approach to teaching EAP that can be adapted to a wide range of postsecondary academic settings, including community colleges, intensive English programs at universities, private language centers, and tutoring programs. We have also aimed to address both language and academic skills. Because English instructors typically have a limited amount of time to prepare students for academic study, they must ensure that they teach both academic English and academic learning. We believe that if teachers can nurture independent learners, students can succeed far beyond the walls of our EAP classrooms.

It is also important for EAP teachers to remember that they are preparing students to participate in a broader academic culture. The American linguist Swales (1990) has used the term "discourse community" to refer to a group of people who share goals, ways of communication and thinking, and social practices. EAP teachers should aim to help English language learners become active members of the academic community in which they are studying. In other words, students are not just learning academic English; they are learning to think like academics and become academics. In addition, if students are studying in a setting that is culturally very different from their native culture, or if they are attending an English-medium university in a country that has different academic expectations than their own, students would greatly benefit from an orientation to the academic culture in which they are studying. As you will see, a recurring theme in this book focuses on making academic practices as salient and accessible for students as possible.

REFLECTIVE BREAK

Think about the academic community in which you work, teach, or study.

- What is the role of language in unifying people in your academic community?

- What is expected of members in this community?

In This Book

In Chapters 2 and 3, we lay the foundation for teaching EAP; Chapter 2 discusses needs assessment, and Chapter 3 outlines general academic skills. In Chapter 4, we discuss academic reading and writing as interconnected processes, and we home in on listening and speaking skills in Chapter 5. In Chapter 6, we illustrate how grammar and vocabulary are intertwined with all four skills, and present examples of two "blended" skills that combine reading, writing, listening, speaking, grammar, and vocabulary. Finally, Chapter 7 emphasizes the importance of reflective practice and continual professional development. As you read, we hope you allow time to use the reflection questions to stimulate your thinking and help you envision how the ideas we discuss may be applicable to the academic setting in which you teach and learn.

2

Needs Assessment

An assessment of learners' needs can help administrators set goals, plan instruction, and design curricula. Conducting a needs assessment is necessary to ensure that EAP instruction aligns with stakeholders' expectations for teaching and learning.

Assessing Stakeholders' Needs

EAP instructors and administrators must ensure that they fulfill the needs and objectives of stakeholders, who may include universities, language programs, and/or national governments. Stakeholders may have explicit, specific goals and expectations for students. For example, a specific goal may be an exact test score (e.g., "Students must achieve an IELTS score of 6 in order to begin full-time academic study"). In contrast, stakeholders' expectations may be implicit and assumed, and program administrators and instructors will need to determine what they are. Unstated expectations may come from language learning myths, cultural differences, or differing interpretations of learning outcomes.

Several tools can be used to formally and informally assess stakeholders' needs, including print and/or electronic questionnaires, interviews, analyses of textbooks and other teaching materials, and classroom observations. Instructors and administrators can also assess what students will need in particular disciplines. For instance, engineering faculty members could be surveyed and asked which skills they believe English language learners in their classes need and/or lack. Having a clear idea of what students will need to do in their majors of study can help EAP instructors adequately prepare them. And like all types of assessment, using different combinations of assessments and assessing continually is important for assuring accuracy (validity) and consistency (reliability).

Assessing stakeholders' needs can also help EAP administrators and instructors identify a mismatch between what students and faculty believe constitutes academic success. For example, at the University of Melbourne, Australia, Ransom, Larcombe, and Baik (2005) surveyed 377 international students about their English learning needs and expectations of university support. Findings show that many international students incorrectly assumed that "language skills will improve significantly solely as a result of participating in English-based classes" (p. 8). Participants also expected their institution to provide significant academic support during their studies. After uncovering this assumption, the authors were able to discuss expectations for learning with students and administrators, suggest positive changes to students' orientation sessions, improve student knowledge about the importance of independent learning, and clarify key points about the impact of "cultural encoding" on teaching and learning. What we learn from this study is that a comprehensive needs assessment can ensure that differences in educational expectations are clarified so students can better understand the academic culture they will be joining.

Assessing Students' Skills and Goals

Large-scale standardized tests such as the Test of English as a Foreign Language (TOEFL), the Test of English for International Communication (TOEIC), and the International English Language Testing System (IELTS) are often used by universities to evaluate students' proficiency and place them into appropriate courses. Once students are placed, instructors can further assess their language skills. For instance, a writing diagnostic given on the first or second day of class can give instructors a sense of students' strengths and weaknesses both as a class and as individual writers. In addition, a diagnostic can provide insight into how students approach writing, including how they plan for writing, organize information and ideas, and revise and edit their work.

Instructors should also gain a sense of students' goals for learning academic English. Doing so can allow instructors to shape their instruction and design materials that align with these goals. For example, a student preparing for graduate work in a science field can benefit from learning how to use reporting verbs (e.g., *explain*, *propose*, or *discuss*, among others) that are frequently found in research reports. In addition, understanding students' motivations can allow instructors to address any myths students have about academic English or language learning more generally. For instance, students might value placement tests over learning because they do not fully understand that EAP instruction builds valuable skills that can take them far beyond test scores and grades. (For an excellent resource on motivating language learners, see Hadfield & Dörnyei, 2013.)

Nevertheless, while students may have very specific goals for learning academic English, they may not always know what their needs are. For instance, a student may require a TOEFL iBT score of 75 to gain admission to his or her university of choice in an English-speaking country. However, this TOEFL iBT score is not what the student actually *needs* in order to succeed at the university after the test is taken. For this reason, it is even more important for instructors and administrators to remain in close communication regarding what students will be expected to be able to do. In this way, we teach both language and academic readiness.

REFLECTIVE BREAK

A student tells you that he achieved a high score on the TOEFL exam and therefore feels that class time will be redundant because he already has what he "needs." How would you respond?

Assessing Local Resources

People tend to think of resources as material items only (e.g., computers or books) and overlook the fact that people are also vital resources. For instance, well-trained and experienced teachers who collaborate to develop innovative teaching techniques can serve as a valuable resource to less experienced teachers. In addition, an informed administration can be a critical resource in ensuring that policies are created based on sound pedagogy and research and not on popular fads and myths. Also, adult students bring a wealth of resources and life experiences that can help promote successful teaching and learning.

Students should be made aware of the resources currently available to them in their local academic setting and know how to access them. As noted, these resources may include support networks of people (e.g., professors, classmates, university writing center consultants, native-speaking conversation partners, and peer reviewers) and academic services (e.g., library help desks or free workshops for students). And as Ransom, Larcombe, and Baik (2005) point out, international students may be unaware of the support services that exist on campus. Ensuring that students are informed about all available resources will only increase their chances of academic success.

Finally, the amount of time teachers have to work with students is also a precious resource. For instance, some intensive English programs (IEPs) have several short terms; some institutions work on a semester-long basis. In some cases, a student may need multiple semesters to develop their academic English skills. For this reason, instructors must think very carefully about the purpose of every assignment, lesson, and assessment so they are able to use instructional time as efficiently as possible.

REFLECTIVE BREAK

- What resources are available in your academic setting?
- How could you work with administration to expand these resources?
- How can you help your students access them?

3

Developing General Academic Skills and Independent Learners

As discussed in Chapter 2, assessing stakeholders' requirements and students' goals will help instructors determine which skills to prioritize in their academic settings. In this chapter, we take a broader look at academic skills and describe those which students need to succeed in all academic settings. We believe that by cultivating confident and independent learners, teachers can help students succeed long after they have left the supportive environment of our EAP classrooms.

> ## REFLECTIVE BREAK
>
> - What kinds of academic skills do your successful students possess?
> - Which skills do your less successful students need?

Which General Academic Skills Do Students Need?

Reading

Reading strategically and purposefully is a crucial academic skill, and students can improve their reading comprehension by learning how academic texts are structured and knowing what to expect in academic genres. With the goal of reading and writing *like* other members of the academic community, students can also benefit from using effective reading strategies, such as top-down and bottom-up skills, to monitor their learning. (For more on teaching reading, see Day, 2013.)

Writing

For academic writing, students must be able to develop a clear line of thinking and support their claims. They also need to produce *coherent* texts that are logically organized, and *cohesive* texts in which ideas, sentences, and paragraphs are connected. Additionally, students will need to produce various types of writing, including research papers; response papers; lab reports; proposals; and both formal and informal e-mails to faculty, staff, administrators, and their peers. They must also borrow from print and electronic texts appropriately by summarizing, paraphrasing, quoting, and citing others' work. Finally, students need to develop their own authoritative "voice" in academic writing and learn to position themselves as knowledgeable members of their academic community.

Listening

Listening in academic settings requires students to comprehend various kinds of discourse. In academic lectures, students must identify key organizing patterns and conventional signal words so they can follow the speaker's line of thinking. To fully comprehend discussions, students need to follow the flow of key points and know when they can appropriately enter a discussion. They should be able to understand what is stated directly and what is implied, follow speech at normal speeds, and resolve any breakdowns in communication. And to maximize their grasp of new content and language, students must understand "teacher talk," the conventional discourse used to conduct classroom business.

Speaking

Speaking in academic settings requires students to clearly communicate their point of view with their peers and instructor, exchange information, and negotiate meaning. One of the most common speaking tasks is oral presentations, for which students need to prepare visual aids to support their delivery of the content, speak with confidence, and manage the flow of conversation in "question and answer" sessions that follow. However, speaking skills go beyond simply giving formal presentations. For instance, in nonlecture classes, students need to become familiar with new types of learning, including problem-based learning, business models, and discovery-learning, and adapt listening and speaking skills appropriately. (For more on teaching speaking, see Bleistein, Smith, & Lewis, 2013.)

Vocabulary and Grammar

Depending on the language learning background of the student, vocabulary study and grammar may be thought of as separate topics. For instance, in some cultures, students are taught to memorize words and grammar rules in isolation from context. However, vocabulary development and grammar knowledge are so important that they are best addressed not as stand-alone issues, but rather as integrated with reading, writing, listening, and speaking. Because English has such a large lexicon, students can easily be slowed down in vocabulary development if they do not have clear strategies for selecting the most useful words and using them in academic language.

Finally, students must realize that there is more to learning grammar than simply memorizing rules; instead, they can benefit from learning grammar through a more dynamic approach, which involves learning to use structures accurately, meaningfully, and appropriately (Larsen-Freeman, 2003). In addition, students can learn to analyze what sentence structures, verb tenses, modals, modifiers, and other grammatical features are used most frequently in their target discipline. Students should develop an awareness of what usage is most common in their particular fields, since academic styles may differ among disciplines.

REFLECTIVE BREAK

- What are some of your favorite ways to develop specific EAP skills?

How Can We Develop Independent Learners? ___

To succeed in new linguistic environments, students need to hone their metacognitive skills, which help them reflect on their cognition (thinking). Metacognitive skills may include strategic reflecting, recognizing, noticing, assessing, identifying, and planning, all of which can help students gain control of their learning processes. Oxford (1996) further distinguishes between learning styles and learning strategies. *Learning styles* can be thought of as general approaches or patterns to solve problems, and can be visual or auditory, intuitive or sensing, or global or analytical. *Learning strategies*, on the other hand, are specific tools or steps that learners take to enhance their language development, whether they are beginning to learn the language or are just practicing it. Language learning strategies may include note-taking, breaking down new vocabulary into separate parts, asking questions, memorizing collocations, or seeking out extended opportunities to practice.

Developing independent language learners means that teachers can encourage students to better understand their own learning styles and strategies. One way they can do so is to help students become aware of the styles and strategies they might already use. For instance, teachers can create interactive speaking activities that allow students to discuss which strategies and styles are common in their countries of origin or are new to them. Table 1 offers some question prompts, sentence starters, and key vocabulary to facilitate students interviewing each other about learning styles and strategies. Teachers can adapt these ideas to their particular population of learners.

Table 1. Sample Interview Questions About Learning Styles and Strategies

Interview questions/ prompts	Sentence starters	Sample vocabulary words
About learning styles		
How do you like to learn new vocabulary?	*I like to use _____ to learn new things.*	• My senses (e.g., eyes, ears) • My emotions • Books • Visual support (e.g., pictures, graphs, charts, tables, or my notes) • Dictionaries • Discussions with my peers • Electronic tools (e.g., my smart phone, computer, or tablet) • Other materials
What is one approach you can use well when learning something new in your academic setting?	*I am good at using _____ to learn something new in academic English.*	
Tell me about a learning style you would like to improve. Why do you want to improve it?	*I'd like to be better at using _____ because _____.*	
About specific learning strategies		
Which new strategies might help you learn?	*I'd like to learn how to _____.*	
What is your favorite learning strategy? Why?	*My favorite learning strategy is _____ because _____.*	• Listening for key words in a lecture • Asking for something to be repeated • Reading headings and subheadings before reading in detail • Memorizing words • Asking questions • Looking for patterns across genres • Drawing visual images (e.g., a graph or mind map) • Taking notes during listening and reading • Working with my classmates or with a tutor
Tell me a common strategy you have learned in school.	*One strategy we learned is _____ .* *When I (read/ write/listen/speak), _____ helps me because _____.*	

4

Reading and Writing Academic Texts

In this chapter, we describe how academic reading and writing are interconnected processes. Smart readers can become smart writers, and if students have a clear sense of their ideas, their writing is likely to be clear as well.

Nonetheless, instructors should remember that individual differences may affect how students learn to read and write academic English. For instance, students within one class may have varying linguistic skills and vocabulary knowledge. They may also have little or extensive experience with academic language either in English or their first language. In addition, students may bring varying cultural expectations and attitudes toward reading and writing, which might be influenced by their families or society. They may also have different motivations for reading and writing and use a wide range of strategies to approach the reading task based on their first language literacy skills (Birch, 2007); as Nergis (2013) has shown, students' awareness of their own reading strategies may help them better understand the texts they read. All of these factors can play a large role in how students approach reading and writing.

Academic Reading

Reading is a complex process that is crucial for students' success. Knowing about students' reading experiences early on can help teachers tailor their instruction to students' needs. For instance, an open-ended survey can provide critical insight into students' experiences and attitudes toward reading. After completing the survey, students can interview each other and ask questions such as: *How much reading (in English) do you do per week? What is the "reading culture" of your country? Of your family?* A class discussion can help highlight similarities and differences in students' experiences and in their prior academic settings.

Another important piece of information that teachers will want to gather from students concerns their reading strategies, because academic reading differs from other kinds of reading. Astute readers understand their own reading strategies so they can adjust them when they encounter any difficulties while reading. Helping students become aware of their reading strategies can provide enormous benefits and help them read academic texts successfully in their other courses.

So how can we develop savvy academic readers? First, we can directly teach effective reading strategies to students and discuss what successful readers do, which may involve modeling tools and approaches to reading. Second, we can help students become aware of the strategies they already use. Students could read a short passage, keep track of their thoughts as they read, and answer the following questions: *How did I prepare to read? What did I do when I got stuck?* Students can then share their answers with the class as the teacher creates a large list on the board, and then collectively analyze patterns.

Before Reading

When preparing to teach reading at any level, it is helpful to think of dividing activities into three main actions. The first step is preparing students for reading *before* they read. Just as athletes stretch and warm up their muscles before a race, students should also stretch their "mental muscles" so they are ready to read and understand the purpose for reading the particular text. Teachers can help students prepare for reading by ensuring that they have the vocabulary they need for the text and are familiar with the topic. Teachers can also show students how to look over the texts quickly, or skim, to gain a sense of how long the text is and how it is organized. Skimming can also help students reflect on what they know already about the topic and help them make predictions about what the text will be about. Overall, prereading activities can engage students in the topic and help them feel confident about the reading task.

During Reading

A second important step is providing structure during the reading process to ensure that students stay on track and read for the right purposes. A common way to help students focus on a text's purpose is to create a graphic organizer, or "the reader's picture of the writer's words" (Flemming, 2008, p. 399). Graphic organizers are commonly used to help students make sense of the texts they read, keep them engaged in reading, and help them remember what they read. They can also help students understand the text and develop original opinions about an idea or ideas in the text. Jiang and Grabe (2007) synthesize important research findings on graphic organizers and provide several examples of ones that can be used for numerous types of written texts.

Table 2 illustrates a graphic organizer used to support students' reading of source-based texts. You can adapt this chart to help students examine short texts (i.e., a paragraph or a news article) or evaluate longer texts that include many sources (i.e., research reports or academic essays). The main point is that students learn to read for a purpose: to learn new information, determine the author's viewpoint, and process new ideas. Students can also see that academic writing has a clear purpose and audience, which reinforces writing instruction.

After Reading

Finally, students should "cool down" after reading and assess what they have learned. Questions that focus on students' comprehension are typical; however, there are additional ways that students can expand on what they have read. At this stage, they can summarize the text or critically respond to it by evaluating an author's argument, extending an author's idea to their lives, applying the main idea to another context, or discussing their opinion of the text. For an excellent resource on reading research, see Grabe and Stoller (2011).

Table 2. Sample Graphic Organizer for Academic Reading

TEXT	What kind of text is it? (e.g., news article, lab report)	Who is the text written for?	Why did the author write it?	What is the main topic of the text?	How is the text structured? Which information comes first?	Which details or information supports this topic? Are there any graphs or tables?

Academic Writing

Within the broad field of academic writing, there is considerable variation in writing across disciplines. For example, engineers may write somewhat differently than linguists in terms of preferred sentence structures, vocabulary, and text organization. Nonetheless, there are core principles that all academic writers must learn, those for which teachers can prepare students.

Teaching About Academic Writing

One way to teach students about academic writing is to provide both effective and ineffective models of academic texts. Model academic texts can give students a better understanding of a text's main elements and purpose. For instance, if students are learning to write an essay, they can examine model essays and dissect their structure by evaluating the purpose of the text and intended audience, analyzing its construction and language use, and discussing how the text is related to other academic texts. Students can also examine how grammar, vocabulary, and language are used in the text. By providing and examining model texts, academic texts become salient to students and help them learn how to construct their own texts.

Teaching Students to Become Academic Writers

Scaffolding writing tasks is important for guiding students step-by-step through the writing process, just as scaffolds temporarily support construction workers working on tall buildings. For example, if students are learning to write a paragraph, they can use templates for support as they learn to write and become familiar with academic genres. Figure 1 provides a sample template that can be used to help beginner writers learn to construct a paragraph. The visual display of information can

Sentence 1: What is the one main topic of the paragraph?
Answer: _____
_____

Supporting sentence 1: What gives the reader more infor- mation about the main topic?
Answer: _____
_____

Supporting sentence 2: What else gives the reader more information about the main topic?
Answer: _____
_____

Supporting sentence 3: What other idea gives the reader more information about the main topic?
Answer: _____
_____

Closing sentence: What should the reader know about the topic before moving on to the next paragraph?
Answer: _____
_____

Figure 1. Sample Template for Writing a Paragraph

help students see how ideas in a paragraph are organized, and students can write their answers directly below the question prompts. They can then use this template to write a paragraph in regular prose.

Writing assignments should also parallel students' abilities. In other words, asking beginner writers to write a lengthy diagnostic essay is not feasible if they have not yet learned how to write a paragraph. Thus, teachers should create assignments that increase in difficulty and complexity and are appropriate for students' levels. In this way, teachers can "spiral up" skills and levels of difficulty in carefully sequenced combinations. For example, you would teach students how to write essays and summaries separately and then combine the two genres later in a summary and response essay, allowing them to see how genres combine to create new genres. (For an excellent resource on teaching academic writing, see Partridge et al., 2009.)

Assessing and Responding to Writing

Formative Assessment

Assessing students' writing is a fundamental component of writing instruction. Teachers can assess students' writing either formatively (during the learning process) or summatively (at the end of the learning process). If teachers assess formatively, then their comments should help writers improve something specific. Ongoing formative assessments may include feedback on drafts and proposals, as well as anything that helps students understand their strengths and weaknesses. There are typically three different sources of feedback: the instructor, the student, and students' peers. Instructors are the primary providers of feedback on students' work; however, students can learn to develop their own review skills and help each other revise their texts.

Teachers need to consider several factors when preparing to give feedback. First, they must think about how they will respond to students' errors. The effectiveness of error correction on improving students' texts has been a controversial topic in the field of second language writing, but overall, research shows it is neither feasible nor useful to address every single error. (For more on this topic, see Ferris & Hedgcock, 2013.) Too much feedback can be confusing and counterproductive, even though students may *want* us to correct every error! Teachers need to decide whether they will respond to students' errors directly or indirectly and whether they will respond to sentence-level errors or larger errors that interfere with meaning.

Second, teachers must consider the timing of feedback. Students should have many opportunities to receive feedback as early as possible in the writing process. What teachers can do is provide feedback to students at varying stages of the process as they brainstorm, develop their ideas, write outlines or proposals, and begin to draft their work. Teachers who are involved in all of these writing stages can help students understand the writing process and feel less frustrated.

Students may also give feedback to each other at varying points of the writing process as peer reviewers. Some teachers have mixed feelings about peer review; they worry that students are not qualified to provide feedback or may be unfocused during the task. Students may also have mixed feelings about peer review and worry about hurting their peers' feelings. Some students do not feel confident enough in their knowledge of English to feel that they are providing valuable feedback, and believe that the teacher is the only one who can and should correct their papers.

Nonetheless, peer review can be beneficial when structured properly because it can help students learn to edit critically. Teachers can help the peer review process run more smoothly by giving students concrete rubrics to fill out while they read each other's work. For instance, questions that are focused on particular parts of the text (e.g., *Does the introduction provide enough background information? Is the thesis clearly stated at the beginning of the paper?*) can provide structure to the peer review process and help students feel more comfortable evaluating writing. Teachers can also conduct a training session with students and walk them through evaluating a sample text. In other words, the class can read the same paper and discuss the paper's strengths and weaknesses. Teachers must remind students to assess the *writing* (not the *writer*) and provide both positive and constructive comments.

REFLECTIVE BREAK

- How would you respond to students who say that they cannot provide adequate feedback because they are "not the teacher" and do not have all the right answers?

Summative Assessment

Summative assessments may include an in-class writing task, portfolios of students' work, or final papers. If teachers assess summatively, they would not expect students to use feedback to make subsequent revisions. Many teachers choose to use a rubric to make sure that they grade each student systematically. You can opt for a holistic rubric, an analytical rubric, or one that includes both holistic and analytical qualities. Rubrics can also be tailored to the particular writing task (e.g., a compare-and-contrast essay) or they can be used to evaluate general writing skills (e.g., organization of ideas). They can also be used to assess speaking activities (see Appendix A for sample analytic and holistic rubrics).

Clear rubrics can help students focus their editing processes and align their text with teachers' expectations. Students should be given rubrics at the beginning of the writing process so they know exactly how their work will be assessed. For this reason, it is crucial that rubrics are written in language that students can easily understand and that all points are clearly explained to students. Teachers outside EAP classrooms may not use a rubric or any kind of checklist to evaluate students' work; therefore, an advantage of using one in an EAP classroom is that students learn how to evaluate their own writing.

Plagiarism

Another major component of academic writing includes borrowing from outside print and electronic sources appropriately and citing these sources using a particular format (e.g., the American Psychological Association [APA] or Modern Language Association [MLA]). If students fail to do so, their text may be considered plagiarism. There is a lot of research on plagiarism in second language writing, and the issue is fairly complex. One important implication from this body of work has been the distinction between plagiarism that assumes cheating with an intent to deceive and "patchwriting," a term which refers to a strategy that inexperienced writers use and is defined as "copying from a source text and then deleting some words, altering grammatical structures, or plugging in one-for-one synonym substitutes" (Howard, 1993, p. 233). This distinction has helped focus on students' writing skills to highlight the necessity of effective instruction.

Instead of focusing on detecting plagiarism, we feel it is much more effective for teachers to focus on teaching students how to borrow from sources. (For a more detailed discussion of research and practice, see Pecorari, 2013.) Nevertheless, teaching about source use involves time, explicit instruction, guided practice, and sensitivity to the complexity of this issue, as students must fully grasp the sentence-level skills that can help them use sources appropriately (i.e., paraphrasing, summarizing, citing, and quoting) and fully understand conceptual notions of authorship, plagiarism, and common knowledge. For this reason, teachers should begin teaching these components of source use in beginner levels and work on these skills as much as possible (for an excellent discussion of teaching source use in all language levels, see Conzett, Martin, & Mitchell, 2010).

REFLECTIVE BREAK

- How is plagiarism viewed in your academic setting? What are the consequences?

- What are other teachers' concerns about plagiarism? How do students feel about it?

5

Listening and Speaking

Listening is an active rather than passive skill. As you will read in this chapter, teachers can use authentic discourse to prepare students for the kinds of listening and speaking skills they will need in academic settings.

Academic Listening

Listening involves both bottom-up and top-down skills. Bottom-up skills may include the processing of sounds, individual words, sentence structures, grammatical structures, and understanding word stress and intonation patterns; in this way, information is processed from the "bottom" (level of language) up to the "top" (meaning). In contrast, top-down skills begin with meaning and mix with the knowledge students bring to the task. These skills may include identifying main ideas and supporting details, making predictions about a topic before or after listening, and determining the meaning of unknown words. Teachers need to help students improve both sets of skills.

REFLECTIVE BREAK

Consider the four activities below. Do they target bottom-up or top-down listening skills? Why do you think so?

Activity 1	Activity 2
• Students attend an extra-curricular lecture given by a guest speaker. They are asked to write down all transition words used by the speaker.	• Students observe a classroom and pay attention to "teacher talk." Students write down any instance of language the teacher uses to frame the class (e.g., "Today in class we are going to . . .")
Activity 3	Activity 4
• Students watch a video clip of a local news story first without sound. They are asked to use visual clues to predict what the story is about. Then students watch the video with sound and discuss the main ideas of the story. They answer questions such as: *What happened? Who was involved? Why did the police arrive late? How will the city address this issue?*	• In class, students listen to a mini-lecture about global warming. After listening once, students are given a worksheet that includes cloze sentences based on vocabulary mentioned in the lecture. After the second listening, students have to list the order in which particular information was mentioned.

In second language research, a view of listening as authentic meaning-making and interaction has replaced outdated behaviorist paradigms that focus only on drills and sound-level decoding (Goh, 2008). Listening is now seen as a skill that involves more than just listening to individual sounds and repeating details. A current approach to teaching listening thus emphasizes developing students' metacognitive knowledge, or understanding of listening processes, and an understanding of the beliefs of themselves as listeners. As Goh (1997) notes, "by encouraging students to reflect on their own cognitive processes, we are helping them to consider for themselves what leads to their success and failure in listening" (p. 368). If students can reflect on their own thinking processes during listening, they are more likely to be successful. They may also feel less anxious during listening, which is important because anxiety may interfere with listening comprehension, particularly in exam settings.

One way to develop students' metacognitive knowledge is to help them understand the listening strategies they already utilize. As we discussed in Chapter 4, teachers can survey students' knowledge of their strategy use, and students can also benefit from discussing their listening strategies with their peers or together as a class. One way that students can keep track of their strategy use is in listening journals; they can orally record their listening activities and then write about them in journals, either during class or at home.

When planning listening instruction, teachers have to think about the kinds of resources available for authentic listening and ask themselves: *What will students need to listen to? Where can I find authentic materials? What kinds of listening texts do I already have access to at my school or university?* One of the most common ways for students to practice listening is in class, where the instructor can provide immediate feedback. There are books available for use in the classroom that include CDs or sound files of lectures. In addition, we can find lectures, podcasts, videos, news reports in audio and video form, and music on the Internet, all of which provide opportunities for authentic listening.

Second, students can practice real-life listening in their academic setting. Such listening tasks might include guest lectures, class lectures, interest group meetings, or other organized campus activities. For instance, students can attend lectures and practice taking notes, listening for meaning, and participating in lectures. An advantage of listening in the real world is that students can see speakers' body language, gestures, and nonverbal communication, all of which facilitate comprehension. In addition, involving students in activities and lectures on campus can help them become more familiar with the university structure, meet new people, and engage in campus life.

Academic Speaking

Speaking in academic settings parallels academic writing in that students need to develop their voice and confidence in articulating their ideas. Students must also be able to communicate in class discussions and oral presentations; work with their peers in and out of class; and converse with faculty, staff, and administrators. (For an excellent textbook that can be used to teach campus communication, see Feak, Reinhart, & Rohlck, 2009.) Faculty from various disciplines may find some speaking tasks more important than others (Ferris & Tagg, 1996), but teachers can prepare students for a variety of general speaking tasks they will need in academic settings.

REFLECTIVE BREAK

- How much do you expect your students to speak in class?

- What criteria do you use to evaluate their speaking skills?

- How do you involve students who are less comfortable speaking in class?

Let us first consider speaking within the classroom, where speaking may take on a variety of forms. First, there may be formal presentation tasks, which students can prepare and practice ahead of time. Speaking and presenting in class may also be spontaneous. For instance, students may be asked to report what their group has found after completing a reading exercise or reviewing homework. Spontaneous speaking may also include hand-raising and speaking out, and students may need to ask for clarification and elaboration during a discussion.

How can we prepare students for classroom speaking? First, it is helpful for students to recognize that there are many parallels between academic writing and academic speaking. As discussed in Chapter 4, in writing it is important to know your audience, have a clear argument, and provide support for your claims. All of these skills apply to speaking as well. For example, a student giving a formal presentation will have to introduce the research topic; give examples; include introduction, body, and conclusion sections; provide support for ideas; and ensure that their presentation is coherent and cohesive (Reinhart, 2013).

Teachers can help students understand the underlying structure of presentations. While there are many types of presentations, Reinhart (2013) lists academic types as including introduction speeches, descriptions and comparisons, concept definitions, problem-solution speeches, and biographical and research presentations. Presenters may also receive feedback on their speaking skills from their classmates. For instance, students in the audience could either fill out a checklist to provide feedback to the presenter or a fill out a worksheet that includes specific questions based on the content of the speech. In this way, students can improve their listening skills and their understanding of academic presentations. Figure 2 provides a sample worksheet that intermediate to advanced-level students can use to evaluate their peers' oral presentations. Teachers can adapt the worksheet to fit their students' proficiency levels or to fit the goals of a particular type of presentation (e.g., a problem-solution presentation).

Students may also need to interact with faculty, tutors, advisers, and staff outside of the classroom in one-on-one settings, and sometimes with their peers in small groups. For example, most faculty hold office hours, which gives students the chance to receive extra help, ask questions, clarify assignment expectations, and discuss course-related matters. Because EAP classes aim to prepare students for authentic university settings, helping students learn to ask for advice and make requests in these out-of-class settings is important. Role-play activities can be effective in helping students understand appropriate academic language for office hours. For instance, students could role play a situation in which they are not happy with their final grade. They might take turns playing the student and the teacher in the interaction, which would help them to gain perspective regarding what goals the instructor might have in such an interaction. Role-plays could then be performed for the class.

Furthermore, real-life observations of mainstream classes can provide students with access to authentic classroom language in their particular academic setting. With the permission of the instructor, English learners may audio-record classroom discourse or take notes on what they observe in the classroom. English teachers may also

Checklist for Presentation Feedback

Presenter's name: _____

Topic:_____

My name: _____

Content
- Did the presenter provide enough supporting details?
- Were all ideas fully developed?

Organization of ideas
- Was it easy or difficult to follow along with the presenter?
- Were ideas organized logically or did the presenter skip around a lot?

Delivery
- Did the presenter make eye contact with audience members or was the presenter reading too much from slides or notes?
- Did the presenter adequately answer the audience's questions after the presentation?
- Did the presenter show enthusiasm for the topic?

Preparation
- Did the presenter know the presentation very well or did it seem like it was done spontaneously?

Visual aids
- Did visual aids help you understand the content?
- Were visual aids helpful or distracting?
- Were visual aids clear and easy to read?

Do you have any unanswered questions?

Presentation's strengths:

Areas the presenter could improve:

Figure 2. Sample Peer Evaluation Checklist for Oral Presentations

provide video-recordings of authentic lectures and prepare teaching materials based on those recordings. Guiding questions might include: *How much do students speak? How does the teacher elicit information from students? Do students work alone or in groups? What kinds of questions do students ask in the class?* Students' notes on their observations could serve as a starting point for class discussions; discussing similarities and differences in teaching styles may help English learners understand how their own expectations vary from those of professors at the university (Leki, 2006).

6

Grammar, Vocabulary, and Blended Skills

Grammar and vocabulary are two indispensable components of listening, speaking, reading, and writing. Note-taking and e-mail writing are two examples of skills that necessitate an effective "blend" of listening, speaking, reading, and/or writing, and are discussed in this chapter.

REFLECTIVE BREAK

- What kind of grammar and vocabulary might be used in academic settings?

- How do you think students like it?

Grammar(ing)

Students often define grammar as the "rules" of a language that must be learned and internalized. While studying grammar does involve studying the rules, language learners need two types of grammar knowledge: knowledge *about* grammar (declarative or explicit knowledge) and knowledge of *how* to do grammar (procedural or implicit knowledge). For instance, a student who has memorized grammar rules but is unable to apply them in communicative contexts can benefit from expanding his or her procedural (implicit) knowledge. Alternatively, a student who communicates in the second language inaccurately and inappropriately, yet can meet his or her communicative needs, can benefit from increasing his or her declarative (explicit) knowledge of grammar. (For in-depth discussion of pedagogical English grammar, see Celce-Murcia & Larsen-Freeman, 1999.)

It can help to consider grammar not as a set of rules, but as a skill that is comparable to reading, writing, listening, and speaking. Larsen-Freeman's (2003) notion of "grammaring" emphasizes *doing* grammar rather than only teaching students *about* grammar. Thinking about grammar as a dynamic process also allows teachers to focus instruction on grammaring, which involves "the ability to use grammar structures accurately, meaningfully, and appropriately" (Larsen-Freeman, 2003, p. 143).

To illustrate the notion of grammaring, see a sample activity in Appendix B. This activity is intended for advanced English language learners and aligns with a grammaring approach that addresses form, meaning, and use of active and passive voice. You can adapt this activity to different language levels by using reading texts that are appropriate to your students' levels.

Vocabulary

Vocabulary is a skill that is fundamentally connected to reading, writing, speaking, listening, and grammaring. Students often believe that learning vocabulary involves the simple memorization of words and their definitions, and they spend a lot of their time memorizing words on index cards. However, learning vocabulary is at all times more complex than learning isolated words. As Folse (2004) notes, vocabulary knowledge includes several components, such as knowing a word's definition and part of speech, frequency, use in context, spelling and pronunciation, possible collocations (or words that typically occur with this word), and possible meanings.

Since the mid-1990s, research on second-language vocabulary learning has proposed that teachers address vocabulary explicitly by providing key words, examples, adequate practice opportunities, and learning accountability through testing. Teaching vocabulary explicitly is particularly important in EAP settings, where time with students is limited. An explicit approach might involve any or all of the following activities: drawing students' attention to new words, writing new words on the board, creating a visual classroom display for new words, and allowing students to use bilingual dictionaries rather than English-English dictionaries.

With so many words in the English language, how do teachers decide which vocabulary to teach? First, teachers can help students recognize and manage high-frequency academic vocabulary then focus on teaching less-frequent words. For EAP teachers, resources such as academic vocabulary textbooks or Coxhead's (2000) *Academic Word List* can help them determine which words are used most frequently in academic discourse. Academic English corpora, or large databases of actual language use, may also be used to complement textbooks that do not address actual language use. (For an excellent pedagogical resource on using corpora to teach English, see Bennett, 2010.)

Students can also benefit from developing working knowledge of other high-frequency lists, such as reporting verbs. (For an excellent research study of reporting verbs in the disciplines, see Hyland, 1999.) Knowledge of this kind of vocabulary not only helps students read source texts, it also helps them to summarize or paraphrase material that they need to write (Schmitt & Schmitt, 2005, p. vi). Lastly, although there is limited research on theme-based vocabulary learning, many teachers find it beneficial to organize vocabulary into related themes to help learners retain new words and understand how they are interrelated.

Students can also be prepared for *incidental* vocabulary learning, which happens when students learn words while focusing on another activity, such as reading. Teachers can help students learn vocabulary incidentally by providing extensive exposure to new words that are appropriate for students' proficiency levels. While this might present a challenge in English as a foreign language settings, where students do not have rich and frequent exposure to English, teachers can still ensure that students have plenty of opportunities to hear and read new words repeatedly. For instance, teachers can create glosses to help students remember new words and understand the meaning of the new word in its context during reading (Ko, 2012).

Because there is a substantial amount of vocabulary that students must learn, and because teachers can only teach so much explicitly, teaching students to manage vocabulary learning on their own is crucial. Promoting effective vocabulary strategy use, for example, can help students learn independently outside of class. A common strategy for guessing the meaning of an unknown word is to use context clues surrounding the word to make an educated guess about its meaning. This strategy can be taught most effectively in the classroom, where teachers can support students' guessing by providing the meaning of potentially unknown words in the context. In addition, students may learn to look for cognates in their first language. Keeping reading and/or listening journals can help students keep track of new words.

REFLECTIVE BREAK

In the chapter introduction, we mentioned that note-taking and writing e-mails are examples of tasks that combine several skills. Before you read the next section, consider what other types of "blended skills" students might need in your academic setting. How might you teach these blended skills most effectively?

Note-Taking

Note-taking can help students interact with listening and/or reading texts, remember what they have read or heard, and determine what they did not understand. Examining students' notes may also give teachers information about their listening proficiency (Song, 2012). Note-taking requires students to concentrate for long periods of time and make inferences, determine main ideas, catch specific details, make real-time decisions about what to write down (for listening), and effectively use their short-term memory.

We can prepare students for note-taking by teaching the skill directly. For instance, we can deconstruct the format of a lecture. Students can learn to rely on micromarkers, which help organize smaller segments of language (i.e., *now, because, on the other hand, as you know*) and larger macromarkers that help organize the overall lecture (i.e., *Today we'll discuss two major problems with...*) to make sense of the content, recognize important information, and follow the speaker more easily.

What's more, providing students with outlines and practicing note-taking as a class can help them become more effective listeners and writers. Notes could take the form of a journal, comments in the margin, lists, outlines, or graphic organizers. Figure 3 displays a double-entry journal, which can be used to support students' note-taking during listening. Students record the main topics in the left-hand column and their notes in the right-hand column. For beginner students, teachers can partially fill out the main topics in advance to provide additional support during the task.

REFLECTIVE BREAK

- Have you ever taken notes in a second language?

- If so, how was the experience different from taking notes in your first language?

- If you have never done so, how do you think you would prepare to take notes?

E-mails

Writing e-mails to faculty, administrators, and peers is another (over-looked) blended skill that is an essential means of communication in academic settings. E-mail writing combines both writing and prag-matic competence (the ability to use language meaningfully for par-ticular functions). E-mails are sent for a variety of purposes: to make requests for appointments, extensions, or recommendation letters; to apologize for missing class; to ask for information; and to send course-work, among other reasons. Students sometimes think that because e-mail can be a fairly informal medium, they can write informal

Main topic	My notes, thoughts, or questions
(TOPIC 1):	
(TOPIC 2):	

Figure 3. Sample Double-Entry Journal for Note-Taking

e-mails to instructors and administrators; however, this is untrue. Several actions that students consider appropriate may be considered rude or informal in an academic setting, such as sending an attachment with no text in the body of the e-mail, using emoticons (☺), using abbreviated language ("thx", "c u tmrw"), not addressing the administrator or professor by his or her title, not including a greeting and closing, and poorly controlling the e-mail's tone. While students may not intend to be rude or may not be aware of these errors, inappropriate e-mails can be offensive to their recipients.

We believe that it is very important to help students understand academic e-mails by making the language, function, and use of e-mail explicit. First, students can analyze sample e-mails to determine the tone, purpose, and language used. Conducting a text analysis of sample e-mails can strengthen students' critical thinking skills and help them better understand this genre. Students could then practice writing e-mails to faculty and compare and contrast their work with their peers. Lastly, teachers can give students the language structures they need to compose e-mails effectively; beginner students can especially benefit from having the language they need to write to their instructors. Discussing e-mail etiquette at the beginning of the course can also clarify your expectations for students and help them feel more comfortable composing e-mails in English.

7

Closing Thoughts

In this book, we hope to have given you a few fundamentals for teaching EAP. We did not intend to present a static one-size-fits-all approach to teaching. All teachers, whether novice or experienced, should strive to grow, critically reflect on their practice, and learn from their students, courses, and teaching experiences. (For a practical guide on reflective practice, see Farrell, 2013.)

We would like to stress the importance of professional development, which keeps educators informed and engaged in the newest pedagogical innovations. Local, national, and international professional TESOL organizations offer countless opportunities for continual growth, including workshops, seminars, publications, advocacy, and networking. Additionally, teachers can invite their colleagues to observe their classrooms. Outsiders often provide insightful feedback and illuminate issues that a teacher may not see. Lastly, teachers can also engage in classroom research of their own to gain on their instructional practices and students' learning. (For an accessible guide on teacher research, see Stewart, 2013.)

Keeping up-to-date with the latest trends in technology use is also critical. As technology rapidly advances and as our world becomes increasingly digital, we can capitalize on the latest cutting-edge pedagogical resources. The Internet provides numerous opportunities for professional growth; for example, teachers can subscribe to English teacher listservs to receive news and updates, find teaching resources, and participate in online seminars.

We hope the ideas presented here have inspired you to delve further into the exciting area of teaching academic English. With the increase of English as the medium of instruction in schools and universities around the world (Doiz, Lasagabaster, & Sierra, 2012), the need for trained EAP professionals is growing. The needs and goals of these students, in addition to the needs and goals of students in our own academic settings, will need to be addressed in EAP teaching and research. The future of professional practice in EAP in the near- and long-term looks dynamic and bright, and there is no better time to become involved in this critically important area of TESOL.

References

Bennett, G. (2010). *Using corpora in the language learning classroom*. Ann Arbor, MI: Michigan University Press.

Birch, B. M. (2007). *English L2 reading: Getting to the bottom* (2nd ed.). Mahwah, NJ: Lawrence Erlbaum.

Bleistein, T., Smith, M. K., & Lewis, M. (2013). *Teaching speaking*. Alexandria, VA: TESOL International Association.

Canagarajah, A. S. (1999). *Resisting linguistic imperialism in English teaching*. Oxford, United Kingdom: Oxford University Press.

Celce-Murcia, M., & Larsen-Freeman, D. (1999). *The grammar book: An ESL/EFL teacher's course* (2nd ed.). Boston, MA: Heinle.

Conzett, J., Martin, M., & Mitchell, M. (2010). Proactively addressing plagiarism and other academic honesty issues with second-language writers. *Writing & Pedagogy, 2*(2), 293–309.

Coxhead, A. (2000). A new academic word list. *TESOL Quarterly, 34*, 213–238.

Day, R. (2013). *Teaching reading*. Alexandria, VA: TESOL International Association.

Doiz, A., Lasagabaster, D., & Sierra, J. M. (Eds.). (2012). *English-medium instruction at universities: Global challenges*. Bristol, UK: Multilingual Matters.

Farrell, T. S. C. (2013). *Reflecting on teaching the four skills: 60 strategies for professional development*. Ann Arbor, MI: University of Michigan Press.

Feak, C. B., Reinhart, S. M., & Rohlck, T. H. (2009). *Academic interactions: Communicating on campus*. Ann Arbor, MI: University of Michigan Press.

Ferris, D., & Hedgcock, J. (2013). *Teaching L2 composition: Purpose, process, and practice*. New York, NY: Routledge.

Ferris, D., & Tagg, T. (1996). Academic listening/speaking tasks for ESL students: Problems, suggestions, and implications. *TESOL Quarterly, 30,* 297–320.

Flemming, L. (2008). *Reading for results* (10th ed.). Boston, MA: Houghton Mifflin.

Folse, K. (2004). *Vocabulary myths*. Ann Arbor, MI: University of Michigan Press.

Goh, C. (1997). Metacognitive awareness and second language listeners. *ELT Journal, 51*(4), 361–369.

Goh, C. (2008). Metacognitive instruction for second language listening development: Theory, practice and research implications. *RELC Journal, 39*(2), 188–213.

Grabe, W., & Stoller, F. L. (2011). *Teaching and researching reading* (2nd ed.). New York, NY: Longman.

Hadfield, J., & Dörnyei, Z. (2013). *Motivating learning*. Harlow, England: Longman.

Howard, R. M. (1993). A plagiarism pentimento. *Journal of Teaching Writing, 11*(3), 233–245.

Hyland, K. (1999). Academic attribution: Citation and the construction of disciplinary knowledge. *Applied Linguistics, 20*(3), 341–367.

Hyland, K., & Hamp-Lyons, L. (2002). EAP: Issues and directions. *Journal of English for Academic Purposes, 1,* 1–12.

Jiang, X., & Grabe, W. (2007). Graphic organizers in reading instruction: Research findings and issues. *Reading in a Foreign Language, 19*(1), 34–55.

Kalpidou, M., Costin, D., & Morris, J. (2011). The relationship between Facebook and the well-being of undergraduate college students. *Cyberpsychology, Behavior, and Social Networking, 14*(4), 183–189.

Ko, M. H. (2012). Glossing and second language vocabulary learning. *TESOL Quarterly, 46,* 56–79.

Larsen-Freeman, D. (2003). *Teaching language: From grammar to grammaring*. Boston, MA: Heinle.

Leki, I. (2006). Negotiating socioacademic relations: English learners' reception by and reaction to college faculty. *Journal of English for Academic Purposes, 5,* 136–152.

Nergis, A. (2013). Exploring the factors that affect reading comprehension of EAP learners. *Journal of English for Academic Purposes, 12*, 1–9.

Oxford, R. (1996). *Language learning strategies around the world: Cross cultural perspectives*. Honolulu, HI: University of Hawaii Press.

Paltridge, B., Harbon, L., Hirsh, D., Shen, H., Stevenson, M., Phakiti, A., & Woodrow, L. (2009). *Teaching academic writing: An introduction for teachers of second language writers*. Ann Arbor, MI: University of Michigan Press.

Pecorari, D. (2013). *Teaching to avoid plagiarism: How to promote good source use*. Berkshire, UK: Open University Press.

Ransom, L., Larcombe, W., & Baik, C. (2005). English language needs and support: International-ESL students' perceptions and expectations. In *Proceedings of the 16th ISANA International Conference, 29 November– 2 December*.

Reinhart, S. (2013). *Giving academic presentations* (2nd ed.). Ann Arbor, MI: University of Michigan Press.

Schmitt, D., & Schmitt, N. (2005). *Focus on vocabulary*. White Plains, NY: Pearson.

Song, M. (2012). Note-taking quality and performance on an L2 academic listening test. *Language Testing, 29*(1), 67–89.

Stewart, T. (2013). *Classroom research for language teachers*. Alexandria, VA: TESOL International Association.

Swales, J. (1990). *Genre analysis: English in academic and research settings*. Cambridge, United Kingdom: Cambridge University Press.

Appendix A: Sample Rubrics

Sample Analytic Rubric for Evaluating an Oral Presentation

	5 (excellent)	4 (very good)	3 (average)	2 (below average)	1 (poor)	Points received
Content	The purpose of the presentation is clear and all claims are supported by evidence.	The purpose of the presentation is clear and there is support for most of the claims made in the presentation.	The purpose of the presentation is somewhat clear. There is support for many of the claims made.	The purpose of the presentation is vague. There is some support for claims made, but many claims are not supported by any kind of evidence.	The purpose of the presentation is not clear and there is little to no support for claims made.	
Organization	The presentation is well organized and logical. It is very easy for the reader to follow the writer's ideas.	The presentation is logically organized. There may be a few ideas that are not logically connected, but most ideas connect back to the main idea of the text.	The presentation is somewhat logically organized, but many ideas are not logically connected.	The organization of the overall presentation is random. Most paragraphs are not cohesive and/or do not connect back to the main idea of the text.	There is little to no organization in the presentation.	
Delivery	The speaker holds the audience's attention and makes eye contact with the audience. The speaker is very enthusiastic about the topic and speaks clearly in an appropriate volume.	The speaker holds the audience's attention for most of the time and makes frequent eye contact. The speaker shows enthusiasm for the topic and speaks clearly and in an appropriate volume.	The speaker holds the audience's attention sporadically and does not make frequent eye contact. There is minimal enthusiasm and the speaker does not speak clearly and/or in an appropriate volume.	The speaker makes minimal eye contact, reads mostly from notes, and shows little enthusiasm for the topic. The speaker does not speak clearly and/or speaks in a low monotonous tone.	The speaker does not make eye contact at all with the audience and shows no interest in the topic. The speaker speaks in a low volume and monotonous tone.	

(Continued on p. 44)

Sample Analytic Rubric for Evaluating an Oral Presentation (continued)

	5 (excellent)	4 (very good)	3 (average)	2 (below average)	1 (poor)	Points received
Visual Support	Visual aids support the content. There is an appropriate amount of support that does not overwhelm the audience.	Visual aids mostly support the content and do not overwhelm the audience.	Visual aids provide some support for the content, but there is either too much or too little support.	The visual aids provide minimal support for the content.	There are few or no visual aids to support the content.	
Mechanics (spelling, grammar, and punctuation)	The visual aids are nearly completely free of mechanical errors. The visual aids align with what the speaker says.	There are a few mechanical errors in the visual aids, but they do not interfere with meaning. The visual aids align with what the speaker says.	There are many mechanical errors in the visual aids that may interfere with meaning, or the visual aids contradict what the speaker says.	There are several mechanical errors in the visual aids that interfere with the meaning.	There are so many mechanical errors in the visual aids that it is nearly impossible to figure out the meaning of the text.	
Comments:						Total points: ___ / 25

Sample Holistic Rubric for
Evaluating an Oral Presentation

	5 Maximum points	Comment
Content		
Organization		
Delivery		
Visual support		
Mechanics		
Total points		

Appendix B: Sample Grammar(ing) Lesson

Objectives	By the end of this lesson, students will be able to summarize a short research article correctly using active and passive voice.
Warm-up (5 minutes)	Using the article, "The Relationship Between Facebook and the Well-Being of Undergraduate College Students" (Kalpidou, Costin, & Morris, 2011): • Teacher previews/teaches new vocabulary with students and discusses the vocabulary in the teacher-created gloss. • Students skim the article and discuss the overall organization of the text. • Students look at the title and guess what the study's hypothesis is. • Class discussion: *Do you use Facebook? Why do you use it? How do college and international students use Facebook?*

(Continued on p. 47)

Activity (40 minutes)	• Students read a short excerpt from a research report and highlight all instances of verbs.
	The relationship between Internet use and loneliness was examined by other researchers too. Moody[6] reported that high levels of Internet use (i.e., time) were associated with low levels of social loneliness (i.e., more social networking) and higher levels of emotional loneliness (i.e., lack of intimate relationships), suggesting that online interactions fail to satisfy one's need for emotional connections in social interactions. More recently, Ceyhan and Ceyhan[7] reported that loneliness and depression predicted problematic use of the Internet, as measured by a scale designed by the authors. To explain the link between loneliness and Internet use, Caplan[8] explored the mediating effect of social anxiety. Indeed, Caplan supported that social anxiety confounded the relationship between Internet use and loneliness and was directly related to negative effects from Internet use.[8] Finally, another variable that seems to moderate the effects of the Internet is how the Internet is used. Non-communicative use of the Internet was shown to influence psychological well-being negatively (i.e., loneliness, depression) because it reduced social integration. Internet use driven by communicative use was positively correlated with psychological well-being because of increased community and social involvement.[9] (Kalpidou, Costin, & Morris, 2011, pp. 183–184)

• Teacher checks comprehension and students go over questions together.
• The class discusses the article's purpose and audience. |

	All active verbs	All passive verbs
	• *reported* • *fail* • *predicted* • *explored* • *supported* • *confounded* • *is/was* • *reduced*	• *was examined by other researchers* • *were associated with* • *was measured by a scale* • *designed by the authors* • *was directly related to* • *is used* • *was shown*

(Continued on p. 48)

Analyze	• Students fill out a chart with two columns. In either column, students list all active verbs and all passive verbs, as demonstrated above. • Students go back to the text and look at how each active verb relates to the "doer" of the action" and how each passive verb relates to the "receiver" of the action. • Students then look at each verb in context and analyze (or discuss) why the author might have chosen to use either active or passive voice in that context. For example, students could address the following questions: Is passive used because the agent is unknown? Or is it not necessary to mention who performed the action? These answers help students focus on meaning and use.
Choosing forms	Look at this part of the passage. If the verb is in active form, change it to passive. If the verb is in passive form, change it to active. Think about which form is better in each instance. Do you agree with the choices made by the original authors? Excerpt *The relationship between Internet use and loneliness was examined by other researchers too. Moody reported that high levels of Internet use (i.e., time) were associated with low levels of social loneliness (i.e., more social networking) and higher levels of emotional loneliness (i.e., lack of intimate relationships), suggesting that online interactions fail to satisfy one's need for emotional connections in social interactions.* (Kalpidou, Costin, & Morris, 2011, p. 183) *The relationship between Internet use and loneliness was examined by other researchers too.* Rewrite in active voice: _____ *Moody reported that high levels of Internet use (i.e., time) were associated with low levels of social loneliness . . . and higher levels of emotional loneliness . . .* Rewrite in active and passive voice: _____

(Continued on p. 49)

Teaching English for Academic Purposes

Using new structures	• Students write a short reflection about loneliness using active and passive forms.
	• Alternatively, a dictogloss could be used in this step, in which the teacher reads a passage out loud (two or three times) and students take notes then collaborate to reconstruct the text using the target grammatical structures. The teacher would choose a similar and less difficult text in which active and passive voice are used.
Cooldown (10–15 minutes)	• Class discussion of personalized questions related to the content (e.g., How do the research findings compare/contrast with what you do on Facebook?)
Homework	• Students write a 250-word summary of a news article or short journal article based on the content students are learning.
	• Students discuss what researchers have said and what is still unknown about the topic. They would use active voice to cite authors, and passive to discuss general ideas about a topic.

REFLECTIVE BREAK

- How were students "grammaring" in this lesson? How were form, meaning, and use addressed in this lesson?

- How might you adapt the idea of "grammaring" to your own teaching context?

Also Available in the English Language Teacher Development Series

. . . AND MORE . . .

www.tesol.org/bookstore
tesolpubs@brightkey.net
Request a copy for review
Request a Distributor Policy